ENDORSEMENTS

Jay Vinson has written a very practical guide that will facilitate your navigating the arduous journey of resilience. This tool will expedite your journey and propel you towards your destiny!

Bishop Dale C. Bronner, D. Min.
Founder/Senior Pastor,
Word of Faith Family Worship Cathedral, Atlanta, Georgia

In his new book, *Moving Past Your Pain*, author Jay Vinson reminds us that although life's adversities are unavoidable, they do not have to derail our destiny journey if we do not allow them to. This book will give you the inspiration and insight needed to help you overcome adversity and reach your full potential.

Michael K. Moore
Lead Pastor, Faith Chapel, Birmingham, Alabama

Jay Vinson's new book will help many who will be inspired by his genuine desire to see people move past adversity into a more purpose-filled life. His examples are backed with biblical truths and facts grounded in real life experiences. I have witnessed him overcome much in his own journey. When he had numerous excuses to find reasons to doubt God's plan, he instead pushed forward toward his destiny, remaining anchored in God's Word while His blessings sustained him. This book is a testament to Jay's perseverance and the fortitude of his faith.

Coach Webster Bumpers
High School Football Coach and Educator
Duluth High School, Duluth, Georgia

Jay Vinson did an outstanding job writing this book. It taps into the mental health arena to build, establish, and advance the kingdom of God. Being open to many people will help them understand that you can go through life with its ups and downs, but with much prayer and faith, you will become more than a conqueror. Keep being a game changer.

Dr. Philander A. Browder
Founder/Lead Servant,
Kingdom Global Ministries International, Clanton, Alabama

This book is an incredible read and edifying encouragement. Pastor Jay has taken the time to be transparent and vulnerable enough to lift others in our evolving living. Fulfillment is more achievable after reading this book.

Apostle Sebastian Holley, Ph.D.
Unity Global Network, Cartersville, Georgia

Although we are spiritual beings, we still live in this natural world and are affected by things in this natural world. When we fail to forget that we are human, holistic creatures, we self-sabotage development in vital areas of our lives. Pastor Jay Vinson has created a blueprint to help guide the reader toward becoming a better version of themselves. He gives meaningful insight on self-care and how the lack of it can lead to physical, mental, social, and psychological complications. Pastor Vinson asks pertinent questions that cause the reader to think critically and realistically about where they are in specific areas of their life. Pastor Vinson has done his research and speaks from a professional perspective of his personal life experiences. Pastor Vinson has created a resource that every leader, coach, consultant, and counselor needs to add to his or her library. Excellently executed!

Dr. Karen Lomax
Founder,
Karen Lomax Ministries International, Inc., Oceanside, California

This book is a great inspiration to those who may be dealing with self-worth or looking for guidance in fulfilling their dreams. Jay has accomplished so many successes while overcoming a great deal of setbacks and detours.

Pastor Sundiata Hudson
Lead Pastor, True Life Church, Villa Rica, Georgia

This book is so impactful. It's amazing that Jay took his life experiences and put it all into this book to help the younger generation. When you read this book, it leaves you no excuse to keep from conquering the world and being brave. Most importantly, put God first in everything you go to do. Jay Vinson really changes the game with this book. I dare you to start reading now for the next shift in your life!

Evangelist Monique Moss
Founder, Kingdom Woman Ministries Inc., Miami, Florida

~~~~~~~~~~~~~~~~~~~~~~~~~~~~~~~~

Jay Vinson went above and beyond in this masterpiece as he provides excellent motivational speaking alliteration in which one will have to pause and assess his or her life. His writings are Spirit-led as he seems to know what to write to hit where the heart is.

Cheeano Cambridge
Radio Personality of "Cheestake," Houston, Texas

MOVING PAST
YOUR
Pain

Making the Journey
Towards Your Destiny

Jay Vinson

Moving Past Your Pain

Copyright © 2023 Jay Vinson

Published by HigherLife Development Services Inc.
PO Box 623307
Oviedo, Florida 32762
www.ahigherlife.com

ISBN: 978-1-958211-41-0 (Paperback)
ISBN: 978-1-958211-42-7 (ebook)
Library of Congress Control Number: 2023905854

Printed in the United States of America.
10 9 8 7 6 5 4 3 2 1

CONTENTS

Introduction

OVERCOMING ADVERSITY

We all go through difficult things in life; *you* will go through difficult things in life. It is critically important that you learn how to overcome any obstacle, adversity, or criticism that may come your way.

Do you see yourself becoming an influential person, entrepreneur, author, football coach, basketball coach, baseball coach, athletic director, student athlete, faith leader, life coach, business owner, or some sort of leader? If you are motivated to become a leader, you must realize that people will judge you for the path you take, not for your destination, which they cannot see. How you handle all the outside noise from critics will determine how successful you will become as a leader.

Before I became a pastor in my junior year in undergraduate school in 2012, I had to overcome the adversity of losing my uncle and my grandmother, who was the pastor at the church where I served for many years. When I became pastor of this amazing church in Tuskegee, Alabama, I heard that I was too young to lead that church, my preaching style was not good enough, and I was not equipped to become an effective leader. After hearing all of this from people I did not even know, I had to focus on what God had called me to do. This focus helped me grow, and I became an author, business owner, philanthropist, youth life coach, spiritual life coach, and an effective leader within the marketplace ministry.

If I could overcome it, you—with God's help—can too.

Life may have dealt you a tough hand, but intentionally using every experience as a growth opportunity will position you to fight through to help others transcend their circumstances to become the people they were born to be.

It is time to remove self-doubt, remove fear, and remove jealousy, to transform pain and become free physically, spiritually, and mentally. Dive into these brief chapters and spend some time pondering the thought questions. Prepare to move past your pain and travel on to your God-given destiny!

Jay Vinson

Part 1

DEPRESSION

KEEP YOUR HEAD UP

In 2020, our entire nation was faced with the plague of COVID-19. Many people battled depression and mental health issues. Most people did not know which way to turn or who to trust. Some even lost hope for life and, most importantly, their faith in God. Issues with depression caused a surge of senseless crimes.

To overcome a private battle with mental health or depression, you must learn how to talk it out with a reliable person who you trust. You must step outside of your comfort zone and whatever keeps you from seeking help. You cannot do life alone.

In the spring and summer of 2020 when everybody was at home due to the global pandemic, I launched a weekly podcast with my best friend from college, Chee Cambridge. We wanted to bring inspiration and hope to our viewers who were losing hope in life and faith in God, who didn't know what to do in life—especially those who were laid off and people who had a vision of starting their own business but were fearful because they did not know if the people they were connected to would support their business.

Before Chee and I started this weekly podcast, we were both working from home and had several conversations about doing something for the people we personally knew and our followers through social media. We launched the first episode of our podcast, "Quarantine: How to Overcome Fear," through Instagram.

We started out with only a few people, but eventually attracted a huge following who would tune in weekly.

Many people wrote to me on a weekly basis, thanking me and telling me how they have been impacted by the different episodes. But the message that encouraged us most in continuing to produce the podcast was sent to us after the very first episode. A gentleman from Florida who I had never met wrote to me, saying that he really enjoyed the podcast and that we gave him a different perspective on life. He had felt like giving up on life altogether, but after hearing all the inspirational words and nuggets that Chee and I shared, his entire mindset and perspective on life shifted for the better.

I responded to his message, thanking him for sharing his testimony with me and for tuning in. I encouraged him to continue to tune in weekly. He did, and he was growing mentally and spiritually. Today, he is doing great things and living out his life purpose. I knew that God had given us a vision that would not only shift our lives, but also would change other people's lives and perspectives, helping them to overcome any obstacle and to always keep their faith in God, even when things were difficult.

No matter what you may be up against right now, you have to always keep your hope built up in God. "So, we fix our eyes not on what is seen, but on what is unseen, since what is seen is temporary, but what is unseen is eternal" (2 Cor. 4:18 NIV).

QUESTIONS

- Are the people you are connected to lifting you up?
- What are you currently battling with?
- Do you feel support from those close to you?
- Do you feel like you need support from a reliable source like a counselor, life coach, or minister?

DO NOT BE DISCOURAGED

You may be a business owner trying to grow your business and it is taking longer than you expected. Never get discouraged or hang your head down. God is working things out behind the scenes, and He is about to position you for greatness. If you just keep a spirit of expectation and continue to scale your business by knowing your purpose, mapping out a business plan and model, mastering your service or product, and establishing a trustworthy team, then watch and see how God is going to send the customers you need.

I took a leap of faith by starting my business in the middle of the pandemic in 2020. Some people asked me, "Why are you starting a business now? Don't you know we are in a pandemic?" I had to block out all the noise and just focus on what God had told me to do. Some people may question what God has spoken concerning your life or has told you to do, but are you going to listen to those individuals, or are you going to listen to God? Keep your eyes forward and your head up. God will connect you with your right target audience which will lead to potential customers.

QUESTIONS

- Has God clearly communicated to you what He wants you to do with your life?
- Are you pursuing that goal single-mindedly?
- What people do you know who can help you avoid discouragement?

HANDLING GRIEF

On February 23, 2020, right before the COVID pandemic arrived in the United States, a 25-year-old African American man by the name of Ahmaud Arbery was murdered in a racially-motivated hate crime while jogging in a neighborhood that was not too far from his house in Brunswick, Georgia. In May 2020, as many Americans worked at home due to the pandemic, video footage of the crime was leaked on the Internet. The video was filmed by one of the gentlemen who was with those who killed Ahmaud Arbery in broad daylight. If it wasn't for the gentleman filming what happened and the video being leaked online, it wouldn't have gained national attention and the men who killed Ahmaud Arbery may have gotten away with the crime.

Many people wonder why this event occurred and why there is so much hate in our world. Two years after this family had to bury their son, grandson, brother, nephew, cousin, and friend, they were able to get closure as all three men were found guilty in the murder of Ahmaud Arbery. After following this case for nearly two years, I knew the family were people of faith, but I pondered how could they keep their heads lifted high after losing their son due to someone who had hate toward someone they did not even know. Even throughout the time of grieving, it will take the parents and the entire family time to overcome this tragedy.

I can remember my mother telling me that her sister was murdered by someone who broke out of prison the year before I was born, and how she found it hard to keep her head lifted high as she was really close to her sister. My mother is a woman of faith, but she still had a difficult time overcoming this pain and moving forward in life. I am sure the parents of Ahmaud feel the same way.

You might have lost a loved one due to senseless crime or a hate crime. Maybe you feel the same way as my mother and Ahmaud Arbery's parents. It is okay to grieve when you lose a loved one. After you have grieved, though, take courage, lift your head back up, and begin to adjust by investing your emotional energy in a healthy and life-giving relationship with a local church. Churches often offer recovery programs if you need one. Set aside time to pray, journal, or reflect on your grief personally.

QUESTIONS

- Do you know someone who has handled grief well? What can you learn from their experience and response?
- Do you have or can you find someone who will commit to walking with you through your grief?
- How can the life of your lost loved one serve as an inspiration for you to continue on the path God has called you to follow?

IGNORING DISCOURAGERS

"But you, LORD, are a shield around me, my glory, the One who lifts my head high" (Ps. 3:3 NIV). Just as David in this text was faced with enemies who mocked him saying that there was no hope for him, you may know people who do not believe in you, and people who look down on you instead of looking up to you. Overcome the discouragement they try to bring. Keep your head up high and stop looking down. People may have mocked you or looked down on you, saying that there is no hope for you. David also had critics who said that there was no hope for him. God is saying that you still have a future, a hope, and a purpose for life if you believe and continue to keep your faith in God.

You may be battling depression due to someone giving up on you or looking down on you. God will bring them back to seek help from you after He takes you places you never imagined. Just continue to keep your hope and faith in God.

QUESTIONS

- What discouraging people in your life do you need to ignore?
- What truths in the Bible counter what the negative people in your life tell you?
- What positive people are in your life who you should pay more attention to?

HOW TO OVERCOME GRIEF

There are downers in this life, but there are also lifters. You will always have people who will down you, but there will also be people who will lift you up. To prosper, you must learn how to live a stress-free life.

When I was a senior in college at Auburn University and did my internship with Georgia State University Athletics, the first people who reached out to me when I moved to Atlanta were my cousins. After spending a lot of time with my cousins while doing my internship, we were able to build a solid relationship like never before, which led to us supporting each other in everything that we set out to do. After my graduation, I landed a job in Atlanta with NBCUniversal Comcast Sports Southeast as a video editor and camera operator. While staying in Atlanta since then, I have built great relationships with a lot of people, but the most authentic relationship was with my family. They have been very supportive in my ministry, my career, and even when I became a business owner in 2020.

My cousin Bobby and I used to spend lots of time together. After his son went to prison, he was very distraught; after all he had done for his son, his son was unappreciative. I would always listen to what my cousin had to tell me about what he was going through and how he wanted to see his son get his life on track. I consistently encouraged him and always left him with inspirational words to keep his head up and know that things will get better. I used social media to spread hope and inspiration as well.

In time, I realized that I was making a huge impact in Cousin Bobby's life. Although he did not attend a local church, he had his own personal relationship with God. As he "liked" and commented on my Facebook content and would interact by leaving a comment on my content, I was encouraged that he was growing in his walk with God. He even occasionally attended our church.

In March 2020, I received word that my cousin had passed away. I took it very hard due to the close relationship that we had developed, especially with him looking up to me as a spiritual leader, but more importantly, treating me like a son.

Have you ever wondered how someone you became close with—a family member, colleague, or a friend—could die unexpectedly? Could the difficult things they were going through have caused deep discouragement, which itself brought on physical sickness? With everything my cousin was going through, he became tired, which brought on a lot of health issues. As I walked through this grief, I had to continue to rely on my faith in God to get me through this difficult moment as well as talk with people that I trusted the most to help me.

My friend, no matter what may come or go, you have to continue to press forward in life. Never keep your head down for long. In due time, pick it back up!

QUESTIONS

- Have you experienced the grieving process before? What did you do well and what could you have done better?
- If you are grieving now, do you have someone you trust to help you through the process?
- Is someone you know grieving? How can you help them?

DON'T QUIT!

I am a former three-sport athlete with my favorite sport being football. I have also worked as a high school football coach, and there have been times when a lot of my former teammates and student athletes would get discouraged about an outcome of a particular game. At times I was discouraged when there were games I thought my team should have won, considering my performance and work ethic while my counterpart was not doing the right things that I was doing. After my team would lose a game which I knew we should have won, I felt distraught, because I never got the amount of playing time that I was informed I would receive from my coach. When I contemplated quitting, my mother encouraged me to never give up and quit, but to always keep my head up by being a hard-fighting soldier, on and off the field. Even after my playing days, I instilled the same wisdom into the student athletes I coached. You should embrace it too.

The Book of Psalms makes it clear that it is important to clearly establish in your heart to seek God in everything you go to do, as David did in Psalm 121:1–2. No matter what adversity you may have gone through in the past or are currently faced with, lift your eyes to the hills, realizing that all your help comes from the Lord. God wants to guide you in everything you go to do in life, whether athletically or academically, but you must truly trust and believe Him in everything you go to do.

My mentee, Joshwa Browder, was a quarterback and defensive back at a private school in Alabama in his freshman and sophomore years of high school, but his father told me that he wanted his son to get more exposure to college recruiters by playing for a high school powerhouse football program in the state of Alabama. Before Joshwa transferred to play for this 7A high school football program, his father had several conversations with the coaching staff to make sure that he was making the right decision for his son by positioning him for greatness. After having several conversations with Joshwa's father about this particular high school, I informed him that it would be a good fit for Joshwa, especially since the type of offense this football program runs fits Joshwa's playing style. So Joshwa ended up transferring to this high school in his junior year and did everything the right way, on and off the field. In the classroom, he stayed focused and maintained over a 3.5 GPA, but he never got all the playing time that had been promised to his father.

Joshwa was a young man of faith whose parents are pastors and leaders within the kingdom of God. He kept his head up throughout all of this, and just by his father seeing something in me, he allowed me to be his mentor. The only thing I could think of was how this young man could have become discouraged and given up altogether, but he kept fighting and putting in the hard work every day.

When he did get playing time his junior year for the junior varsity and varsity team, he gave it his all and outperformed everyone. Going into his senior year, he stayed focused and trained with one of the elite quarterback coaches in Birmingham, Alabama. After training tirelessly in the offseason with this elite quarterback coach, Joshwa made tremendous progress at being a proficient quarterback, just to get word that he would not become the starting quarterback his senior year.

The 2022 season was Joshwa's final season as a high school student athlete. The team had its ups and downs through the season. I sent Joshwa motivational and inspirational text messages periodically throughout the season to encourage him to always be ready when his number is called, to take advantage of the moment by giving it his all and leaving it all on the field.

Several times, he was called on, whether for a play or two or an entire series on offense. One Thursday night, there was a home game where it was pouring down rain the whole time. Joshwa was given the opportunity to start. He played one of his best games, but in the fourth quarter on offense, Joshwa was leading his team down field to potentially win the game, but he ended up fumbling the ball as the rain began to pour. One of the opposing players scooped up the ball and ran it back for a touchdown. The visiting team won.

The next day, there were death threats made toward Joshwa at school from students and through social media for losing the game. After I received word about this, the only thing I could think of was not the game's outcome, but more importantly, Joshwa's state of mind. After losing the game, even after receiving several death threats, there was no one to embrace or console him. As Joshwa's mentor, his family and I made sure that he was still

19

doing well, mentally, spiritually, and psychological. He did go into depression mode, but with his family and I being people of faith, we not only kept him in prayer, but we kept encouraging, uplifting, and talking to him daily. He soon came around and got back on track and on top of his game.

Although Joshwa's senior season did not go the way he wanted it to, and he may have even contemplated quitting and walking away from football altogether, he still bounced back and held his head up.

QUESTIONS

- What difficult experiences in life have caused you to contemplate quitting? How did you overcome them?
- Is it ever appropriate to quit? If so, when and why?
- How can you relate in an upbuilding way to someone like Joshwa who is going through a discouraging experience?

TOXIC OR THERAPEUTIC?

Throughout the 2022 collegiate football season, there was one team that took college football by storm. It was not even a power five school; their name is Jackson State University. They had a remarkable 2022 season, and they had been a good team over the previous two seasons. Their head football coach was Deion Sanders, also known as Coach Prime. His squad really took college football by storm, as he had a lot of players who transferred from power five schools like University of Tennessee, Ohio State University, University of Florida, University of South Carolina, Marshall University, and many more. But the 2022 season was special. They hosted ESPN College GameDay, went undefeated during the regular season, and even won their conference the Cricket Southwestern Athletic Conference Championship against Southern University. Right before their final game of the season, which was the Cricket Celebration Bowl game against North Carolina Central on December 17, 2022, a power five school, Colorado University, announced Deion Sanders as Head Football Coach.

After becoming the head coach at Colorado, Coach Prime had to juggle two things at once by making sure that his team at Jackson State stayed focus throughout their postseason bowl practice leading up to their bowl game and having to take on different tasks at Colorado. Throughout this entire process,

Jackson State players had to remain focused on the tall task that was ahead of them and their goal of going undefeated for the 2022 football season. As Coach Prime entered his final game as Jackson State University football head coach against North Carolina Central, both teams put on a tremendous game, which was aired worldwide on ESPN. As both teams went back and forth throughout four quarters, the game ended up going into overtime. Jackson State ended up losing after their talented tight end dropped a would-be game-tying touchdown in overtime.

Shortly after the game, several players were disappointed at losing the game, as they all wanted to go out as winners. But the most disappointed player was none other than the talented tight end who dropped the game-tying touchdown. He had to be consoled in the locker room by former head coach Deion Sanders, who let him know that it wasn't his fault and he'd done good things all season.

In a video that went viral on social media, Coach Prime informed this player that the drop pass was not on him; it was on everybody. He even told this talented student athlete, "I need you to fight through this adversity. This is going to prepare you for life, and that moment is going to make you be one of the best for the rest of your life." As that video went viral, it showed how the former Jackson State head coach not only wanted to win the game, but how he cared deeply for his players—not just by consoling this young guy, but by caring for his mental state, which means so much to every student athlete.

The next day, Sunday, December 18, 2022, my former pastor, Dr. E. Dewey Smith of the House of Hope Atlanta, posted on his social media that he had gone to the Celebration Bowl game to show support to his friend Coach Deion Sanders. But, in doing so, he was there to speak life into and console this talented tight end right after the game. Even though this student athlete was inconsolable for hours, Dr. Smith posted a photo of himself in the locker room, ministering to and praying for this student athlete. Dr. Smith said that God had him there at the game for a reason and purpose and that was to minister to that young man's pain and pray for him. "The righteous cry out, and the LORD hears them; he delivers them from all their troubles. The Lord is close to the brokenhearted and saves those who are crushed in spirit" (Ps. 34:17–18 NIV).

While he was in the locker room, this young man's mother and girlfriend received numerous threatening messages from anonymous sources. The messages became so bad they had to hide in the bathroom until the stadium was empty.

We live in a world where people run to social media every minute, hour, or multiple times a day, expressing their feelings about any trending topic. But people often forget that these student athletes are human and have lives outside of athletics. You never know what a student athlete may be going through internally. Every student athlete needs to have someone who will encourage them, speak life into them, and even coach them outside of athletics. That's why it is very important for every student athlete to have a personal or success life coach as well as a counselor who will help guide them if they are battling anything alone and may not feel comfortable discussing their issues with their athletic coach.

QUESTIONS

- Is your use of social media upbuilding to others, or detrimental?
- How can you have a positive impact on others who you may not know personally?
- How can you encourage others to keep matters in correct perspective and proportion?

STRESS

What causes you to lose sleep at night? After coaching several people and hearing their stories about how they are so stressed out over a particular relationship, breakup, failed friendship, or failed marriage, they tend to become so stressed out over these things that they have no hope or purpose for life. But God does not want you to live a tired and stressful life. He wants you to live a life full of abundance and prosperity. To do that, you have to learn how to bounce back from any failed relationship instead of keeping your head down.

Statistics show that 110 million people die every year as a direct result of stress. That is seven people every two seconds. The most-stressed age group is Millennials (ages 18 to 33), and Gen Xers (ages 34 to 47) report the highest average stress levels. Boomers (48 to 66) and Matures (67 years and older) join them in reporting stress levels that are higher than they consider healthy.

To relieve stress, you must learn how to stay active and relax your mind. Here are ten ways you can work to relieve stress.

1. Find music that is uplifting and positive.
2. Talk it out with a reliable friend who you trust and can vent to.
3. Talk yourself through it.
4. Eat healthy.
5. Laugh certain things off.

6. Drink green tea.
7. Be mindful of the company you keep.
8. Exercise daily—walking, running, weight training, etc.
9. Get enough rest each night.
10. Breathe easy.

QUESTIONS

- What causes you to stay in an unhealthy relationship?
- Do you have a "self-care day" occasionally? What does it consist of?
- When was the last time you had a self-care day?

SUICIDAL THOUGHTS

If you do not adequately handle stress, it can get out of hand and cause you to think about taking your own life. There have been a lot of influential people who have died by suicide. Many factors can lead to this, such as mental health issues. In 2022, many student athletes and celebrities revealed battles with mental health and how they needed to take a break from playing sports or being involved in any activities that may cost them their peace or healthy mental state.

Being in ministry since my teen years and currently pastoring, I have seen many faith leaders put their entire emphasis on ministry and forget to enjoy the life that God had given them. This caused them to become burned out and tired. Even operating in marketplace ministry, such as school teaching, can lead to burnout and exhaustion.

To avoid this, it is very important to take a vacation or sabbatical to be fully charged up for your return. If you have been in a bad relationship, give yourself time to heal. Constantly getting the same results gives the enemy an opportunity to introduce the idea that you do not have anything to live for. "Lift up your heads, you gates; be lifted up, ancient doors, that the King of glory may come in" (Ps. 24:7 NIV). My friend, you have so much to live for and a purpose to fulfill on this earth while you are alive! Do not let a bad relationship cause you to contemplate ruining everything that God has planned for your life. The apostle Paul encourages you to pray, "lifting up holy hands" (1 Tim. 2:8 NIV). When people disappoint you, instead of becoming discouraged and depressed, God wants you to decide to lift up your head and eyes and look at the possibilities, not the problems, around you, trusting Him to lead you into an even better situation. He does have one for you!

As a former Production Assistant working behind the scenes in the television and film industry, I know such work can become overwhelming and tiring. In December 2022, a gentleman from my hometown of Montgomery, Alabama, by the name of Stephen Boss, also known as DJ tWitch, committed suicide. He was well-liked by everyone, even during his time of working on the Ellen DeGeneres show as the DJ. A lot of people and even Ellen said he was very humble and always had a smile that would light up a room. Not only was he from my hometown, but we both graduated from the same high school in two different graduating classes.

One of my church leaders knew him and his family well. He was devastated by the news, as he had great things to say about DJ tWitch. I had the privilege of working in production during a summer camp with one of DJ tWitch's mentors, Dr. Tonea Stewart, who is an American actress and former professor and dean of the College of Visual and Performing Arts for Alabama State University. After she learned of the news of his death she admitted, "It's strangeness and it's a heavy feeling on the insides." The entire world was heartbroken to learn of this young man taking his own life, as he was full of life, purpose, and love, and had a heart of giving to other people.

You never know what someone may be going through internally, although they may have a smile on their face and may be doing all the right things externally. That's why it is very important to check on your loved ones on a consistent basis to see how they are doing and to have those tough conversations, because you never know if someone is battling depression alone, hiding behind a smile. Listen very closely to what someone may be saying to you, whether on the phone or through a text message or other form of communication. Four days before his death, he messaged his grandfather that he loved him and even posted a birthday message on his social media. Although he left behind a suicide note that alluded to his past challenges, tWitch showed no signs of depression, so no one knew why he did what he did.

If you are battling depression or contemplating suicide, please realize that you can overcome these things, but it is very crucial that you get the help that you need from a reliable source. You must recognize that you have a real enemy whose mission is to steal, kill, and destroy. But Christ came to give abundant life and joy. "The thief comes only to steal and kill and destroy. I came that they may have life and have it abundantly" (John 10:10 ESV).

You must choose not to be driven by fear. You might be a business owner, educator, faith leader, musical artist, producer, director, DJ, or any person of influence, but don't be afraid to reach out and help someone who is struggling, or to reach out for help if you find yourself struggling. God won't ever let you go. He has given you others in life to help shoulder your burden. There is support and counsel available from many who understand or have walked this road before. My friend, you must know that you're never alone. God offers hope and deliverance. "The Lord is near to the brokenhearted and saves the crushed in spirit. Many are the afflictions of the righteous, but the Lord delivers him out of them all" (Ps. 34:18–19 ESV).

Even if some people never showed you love the way you wanted them to, just know that God loves you and is always with you until the end of time. He will sustain you through your greatest trials. Whatever you may be facing right now, no matter how dark it may seem, you will not remain the same. There's hope ahead. "For I know the plans I have for you, declares the LORD, plans for welfare and not for evil, to give you a future and a hope" (Jer. 29:11 ESV). Isaiah 55:11 says there is power in God's Word. Praying it back to Him is powerful. God's Word won't return void, without accomplishing great things. Even in your deepest struggles, just know that God can bring you through any mental health state or depression. He will bring you through the other side, by His healing and strength.

No matter how your life has turned out or how it may be presently, you have two options: either give up and quit, or keep going. If you decide to keep going, again you have only two choices: live in depression and misery, or live in hope, joy, freedom, peace, abundance, and prosperity. Choosing to live in hope, joy, freedom, peace, abundance, and prosperity does not mean that you will not face any more disappointments or discouraging situations; it just means that you have decided not to let them get you down. Instead, you will lift your eyes, hands, and heart and not look at your problems, but at the Lord who has promised to see you through abundance and victory.

QUESTIONS

- What are some things you are currently dealing with?
- Are you at peace in life?
- What is your life purpose?
- When was the last time you took a vacation or sabbatical?

Part 2

WATCH YOUR MOUTH

WORDS HAVE POWER

Right this moment, I am living out my dream.

I had some setbacks in life, all because of the words I used to speak. When I was in high school struggling with the high school graduation exam, I would speak negatively of the graduation exam. My parents told me to have a positive outlook on life and the things I was doing. Throughout my high school time as a student athlete involved with Fellowship Christian Athlete and other clubs at school, I still struggled with my graduation exam until my senior year. My mindset eventually changed for the better, and I began to speak positive words about passing this last part of the graduation exam. After speaking positive words, praying to God, and trusting Him, He answered my prayers by letting me pass this graduation exam my last time three months before my high school graduation.

You may be going through some difficult or challenging things in your personal life. You must learn how to speak positive things rather than negative things. If you keep a positive mindset, you will always receive a positive outcome. "Death and life are in the power of the tongue, and those who love it and indulge it will eat its fruit and bear the consequences of their words" (Prov. 18:21 AMP). In everything that you go to do in life, you have to speak life over any dead situation. If your children are struggling academically, speak life over them. If your children are student athletes and had a bad practice or game, speak life into them. Every time you speak life into your children's lives, you will begin to see how they will be encouraged by the words you are speaking over them. You will see how their character will develop as well as how they will become better students and athletes—but most importantly, better people.

The thing I love most about being a mentor and youth life coach is that I get to see young people develop and grow within their craft and gift that God has given them. But more importantly, I get to see them grow into better young men and women. I mentored a great young man who loves God, his family, and football. In 2020, I had the pleasure of connecting with his father, who is an apostle in the state of Alabama, and since we have become brothers and family. He allowed me to mentor his son, who is an honors high school student and is on track to graduate high school with the class of 2023. What I love about his son is not only is he a smart and bright young man, but he is also a hard worker and gifted athlete who plays football just like I did when I was in school. After meeting him and mentoring him, the thing that stuck with me was how humble this young man was and how he listened to everything I would speak in his life. I would always send him encouraging words right before a game, and even with the setbacks he had in his senior year of playing high school football, he never lost his hope in God and he overcame a lot of adversity.

To soar or become great in life, you cannot entertain negative people. If you are ready to go to the next level in life where God wants to take you, it is crucial to speak positive words and sur-round yourself with positive people who will speak life into you when you are doing good, doing bad, and even when you feel like giving up altogether. You may have heard the phrase "you are going to have to eat your words," and Proverbs 18:21 confirms this truth. The words you speak have power to influence your life. In most of my speaking engagements, social media posts, or platforms that I am invited on, I speak positive, uplifting, and inspirational words, and those who hear those words receive life in their relationships, in their ministries, in their thoughts, and in all the areas that God uses me to speak to them.

QUESTIONS

- Are you an inspiration to others? Why or why not?
- Who inspires you and why?
- Are you speaking life over yourself daily?

Part 3

BORN TO WIN

YOU WERE CREATED TO BE A WINNER

As I read the Book of Acts, I am reminded of the Apostle Paul's great leadership traits. The first trait is being humble. Whatever you are trying to do in life, you should never think highly of yourself or think you are better than the next person. If you always show humility, you will see how God will exalt you and let you accomplish everything that you have laid out to accomplish.

Just as the Apostle Paul was humble, he also had a servant heart. You may be serving in a leadership capacity in church, school, sports, or business. In any leadership capacity, you must have a heart for the people you serve, with the right motivation—for God's will to be accomplished. If you have the right heart to serve others before your own needs, without expecting anything in return, then you will begin to see how God will let you flourish as an effective leader, and you will see those you are serving begin to grow.

"Serving the Lord with all humility of mind, and with many tears, and temptations, which befell me by the lying in wait of the Jews" (Acts 20:19 KJV). Have you ever considered how easy it is to forget that the most effective way to share your faith is to live it out? Nothing you can ever say can witness as powerfully to God's power as the changes you can see in your life. What are you doing for the young people in your life—your own children, or others you relate to—to invest in their lives and to prepare them to be leaders who refuse to be mediocre?

For youth to be successful in life, they must learn how to use their voice correctly, to be respectful toward their teachers, parents, grandparents, or any adult in authority over them. Being respectful toward any adult will take any young person farther in life and they will be able to find favor with other people. As a young boy growing up, my parents instilled in me to be respectful and polite to any adult or person that I met and to never be disrespectful. Just by doing that, I was able to find favor with other people and set great examples for my peers. As a believer in the kingdom of God, people are going to compare what you say with how your life has been transformed. For instance, what you say must be encouraging, uplifting, and inspirational, encouraging to everyone you meet. If you are constantly negative, people will not want to be bothered with you or support you. It is very important to set positive examples for others who are around you. If you do that, you will make a huge impact in those individual lives, causing them to want to become great in life.

QUESTIONS

- Are you speaking positive words?
- Do you love God, life, and people?
- Do you treat your coworkers, employees, teammates, or leadership team with respect?

WISE DECISION-MAKING

As a leader, the worst thing that you can do is to get caught up with the wrong individual who may lead to destruction and cause you to lose everything that you have worked so hard to build. In anything that you do in life, you have to pray to God first to make sure that you are making the right decision. You must learn how to follow God when He tells you to do something. If you do that, you will begin to see how your career will become successful. If God is taking you to another level in life, you must be mindful that God will remove some people out of your life who may be harming you, physically or spiritually. When God does that, you must understand that he wants to free you from certain people or certain things, but you cannot hold onto them; you have to learn how to let them go. Once you begin to let them go, you will begin to see how you will grow spiritually and how God will place the right people in your life.

HOMEWORK

1. Do one thing this week to get you closer to making a good, sound decision by evaluating your options and priorities for reaching your goals.
2. Identify the critical factors which will affect the outcome of your decision.

3. Gather information that will help you make the right decision.
4. Identify alternative options.

QUESTIONS

- Do you find it hard to make good, sound decisions?
- What are some things that are hindering you from following God?
- What are some things you are praying to God for?
- Are you afraid of letting go of certain people?

LOVE

Another step of faith for living in the kingdom of God is to love people from all walks of life. God's greatest commandment is for you to love one another. It does not matter how much you dislike a person; if that person has done you wrong, or spoken evil of you, you still must love that person.

I once knew a person who was a believer, but they always talked bad about another person because they did not like how that person treated them. I had to remind that individual to love that person no matter how bad they treated you. At first, they did not want to love that person, but they thought about it and eventually loved the other person. I learned that you can still love a person, but you can love them from a distance, especially if there is no purpose to remain friends with a person who has done you wrong.

Deuteronomy 6:5 says, "You shall love the Lord your God with all your heart and with all your soul and with all your might" (ESV). In order to continue to grow in love everyday spiritually you have to love God first, secondly love yourself, and thirdly love others. You may be operating a rapidly-growing business and you want to expand. Before you expand your team, make sure that your love is patient and kind, so that the people you plan on hiring to your team can feel the love and warm welcome to be a part of your brand and business. That is very crucial to operating a five-star thriving business, not just locally, but globally.

HOMEWORK

1. Do something this week for someone you do not know and ask for nothing in return.
2. Do one good thing for someone you know who doesn't like you.
3. Call a family member this week who you have not spoken to in a long time.
4. Support your friend or family member's business throughout this year.
5. Take your team out for lunch or dinner this month for all their hard work they put into the business.

QUESTIONS

- Do you love God just like you love people?
- Will you show love towards everyone, even when you don't feel like it?
- What is causing you not to love people?
- Do you find it hard to love people who have constantly done you wrong?
- Do you treat your coworkers, employees, teammates, or leadership team with respect and love?

FAITH

When I was growing up, my pastor would frequently say that faith is the size of a mustard seed and it is the substance of things hoped for, and the evidence of things not seen. When I became a leader in the faith and a leader in marketplace ministry, I learned that whatever you go through in life, you must trust the process that God carries you through. If you can trust the process that God carries you through, then you will begin to see how your faith has increased.

Has there been a time when you put your entire trust or confidence in someone, just to find out that they let you down or left you hanging? You may have connections, friendships, and relationships with people, but to be successful, you must make sure that those relationships are genuine, authentic, and real. Some relationships may not last as long as you expect, but you must continue to trust God throughout the process. There are seasons in life, and some relationships may run their course in a season or two. Don't lose faith in what God is trying to do in your life.

Faith requires sacrifice. What are you willing to sacrifice to go to the next level in life? To give God your best, you must spend more time with Him, and once you begin to spend more time with Him through prayer and reading His Word, you will begin to see how your faith will increase when you are going through adversity. You will begin to see how God will take you to the next level in life if you stay connected with Him.

What would be the purpose of living in mediocrity? Doing great things gives God glory, and it is what He wants. God wants to do great things through you. You must learn how to embrace this reality and start dreaming bigger, and you will realize that God is a God of multiplication. In other words, when you think *God*, think *more*. Whatever God has given you, He expects you to share with others, so that it can multiply. When you start in faith, God will finish with abundance and prosperity.

QUESTIONS

- What are you dreaming?
- Are you dreaming big or small?
- Are you living a faith-filled life?

Part 4

SERVANT HEART

WHAT DRIVES YOU DAILY?

The Bible says, "He gives strength to the weary and increases the power of the weak. Even youths grow tired and weary, and young men stumble and fall" (Isa. 40:29–30 NIV). God knows everything and understands all your pain. There is nothing He doesn't know. You may get tired of trying to do right and want to give up and go back to old habits. If you endure and keep faith in God, He will renew your strength so that you can continue.

Carnell Cadillac Williams, the popular interim head football coach at Auburn University, took over once the previous head coach was let go after two seasons. The team was on a five-game losing streak before running back Coach Cadillac took over. My older brother, Don Timmons, played football at Auburn with Coach Cadillac. I even had the privilege of being Coach Cadillac's colleague with the University of West Georgia football program for one season as a graduate student in 2016. The thing that stood out to me the most was Cadillac's drive to become a better position coach and shape all his guys to be great men, on and off the field. As an Auburn alum, I was happy when Coach Cadillac became Auburn's running back coach in 2019 under former head coach Gus Malzahn. I knew that Auburn had a prolific and great running back coach.

Not only was he driven every day to become great, he was driven to become a better learner. He was always a great athlete on the field, from his playing days at Auburn and his time in the NFL with the Tampa Bay Buccaneers, but now he is destined to become a great coach. Although he took over as the interim head coach, he was the first African American head football coach in Auburn history. Ever since he took over, he brought a new energy to the football program, although fans (and I) did not see it for a while.

Before coaching his first game as interim head coach, Coach Cadillac admitted how scared he was to take over the team, and he wasn't afraid to let his team know. He became the interim head coach on Halloween, October 31, 2022. After losing his first game as interim head coach, he said he was scared as a puppy. Even though his team lost, he liked the way they fought and played the entire game.

After his first game as interim head coach, his team won two games in a row before losing their last game of the season against in-state rival University of Alabama. Under his watch as the interim head coach, he was 2-2 as the team ended the season 5-7.

The thing I loved about Coach Cadillac was how he always gave credit to God first and how he always talked about leading by example through serving, being disciplined, and believing. Most importantly, all his guys fed off the passion and energy that he brought to his team, and they played hard the rest of the season for their coach, football program, and university. During his final post-game press conference as interim head coach after losing to the University of Alabama, Coach Cadillac revealed that twelve players had given their lives to God. That just goes on to show the impact that Coach Carnell "Cadillac" Williams had on his players as a man of faith and integrity during his short time as interim head coach.

QUESTIONS

- What is your *why*?
- What wakes you up every day?
- What motivates you daily?
- Are you passionate about what you do?

FATIGUE

It seems that most people in the world today are tired. Part of being fatigued and tired comes from being too busy, but another large part of it is due to the way you live, how you think, talk, and act toward other people. Have you wondered why you are so drained, tired, and not energized? Could it be due to not getting enough sleep daily, lack of energy and motivation, unhealthy eating habits, lack of physical activity, and emotional stress?

Many times, I have been energized by the Holy Spirit and have suddenly gone from being extremely tired to feeling as though I could run a marathon. If you keep yourself filled with the Holy Spirit, you will have all the energy you can get. That's why it is important to keep yourself in a positive state of mind, because if you think negatively and talk negatively, you will drain yourself. Whatever you want to do in life, you have to wake up with a purpose and for a purpose. To know what your purpose is in life, you must know what God has called you to do on this earth. The Holy Spirit will not energize you to be mean, hateful, selfish, or self-centered. He will give you strength and energy to do the things that He has called you to do, and to be kind, loving, diligent, and focused on the process. If you learn how to rest on God's promises, you will see how your body and mind will be renewed and how everything will shift in your favor.

Sometimes when you start to get nervous and upset, anxious, or worried, you just need to tell yourself to sit down. That does not mean just your physical body; it also means your soul, mind, will, and emotions. It is very important to let your entire being rest. If you are struggling in your life, take a seat and rest in the presence of God. The promise of God's peace is not made to those who work and struggle in their own strength, but to those who sit and rest in Christ Jesus. Wait on Him, and your strength will be renewed.

QUESTIONS

- Are you letting people burn you out with their problems? If so, why?
- Is self-care important to you? If so, why?
- Do you find it hard to wait on God? If so, why?

Part 5

FORGIVENESS AND RECONCILIATION

WHY FORGIVENESS IS IMPORTANT

In Matthew 22:37–40, Jesus instructs: "Thou shalt love the Lord thy God with all thy heart, and with all thy soul, and with all thy mind. This is the first and great commandment. And the second is like unto it, Thou shalt love thy neighbor as thyself. On these two commandments hang all the law and the prophets" (KJV). Anything that violates those two key commandments is a sin. You may have done something wrong which caused you to lose your job, gone through a painful breakup, or lost a loved one due to a senseless crime, sickness, or unexpected death. But you may have disappointed your family or friends after losing your job, which caused them not to forgive you for your mistakes. Maybe you find it hard to forgive those who spread rumors and lies about you or a loved one. For you to show grace, you first must learn how to forgive those who are slandering your name and still love them from a distance.

Is it hard for you to forgive? Use this checklist of Reflection Questions to find out.

- Has someone hurt you in the past, and are you still holding on to that hurt?
- Is there someone in your past, alive or dead, who you have not forgiven for hurting you?
- Do you have a hard time going to someone you hurt in the past to ask for forgiveness?
- Do you feel too proud to ask for forgiveness?
- When you feel bad, do you try to make others feel bad or sorry for you?

If you cannot forgive, you cannot sustain love. If you do that, my friend, you will be able to eventually move forward in life, but you must understand that there will be times in your life where you will have to constantly love and forgive people who may do you wrong.

QUESTIONS

- When was the last time you forgave someone and what was the outcome?
- Do you show grace towards people who may have mistreated you?
- Do you find it hard to forgive people over and over again?

THE NEED FOR FORGIVENESS

When you commit a sin, you put up a wall between yourself and God. God loves you deeply, but He hates sin so much that it causes separation between man and God. Your sins are so great that you cannot possibly pay for them. The good news is that His love for you is so great that He sent His only begotten Son, Jesus, to die on the cross as payment for your sins. The only way your sins can be forgiven is for you to receive the gift that His Son has given you on the cross.

On December 5, 2011, the University of Mississippi football program, also known as Ole Miss, hired a head coach to lead their football program. He led the football team to three consecutive bowl games, and even won the 2014 Grant Teaff Coach of the Year award by the Fellowship of Christian Athletes. But in January 2016, the NCAA charged Ole Miss with numerous recruiting violations and forced Ole Miss to vacate wins. Twenty-seven of those wins were under this coach's leadership. He was given the option of resigning or getting fired, so he resigned in 2017.

After all the allegations and the recruiting violations, what stood out to me was how the coach had to ask for forgiveness from the ones close to him who he let down, especially his wife and children. As he was and still is a man of faith, he knew that he had to ask God for forgiveness for all the things that he did that were terrible; they could have destroyed his entire character, reputation, and his family. But, by forgiveness, love, reconciliation, and God's grace, he was able to bounce back.

On December 7, 2018, this same coach was named Liberty University Football head coach. During his time at Liberty, which is known for its divinity school, he was able to get things back on track, on and off the field. Most importantly, he was able to get his relationship with God back on track. While some people may still hold things against him due to what happened at Ole Miss, the thing I love about God is that He will still love you despite your mess, and He is able to forgive.

To move forward with your life, you must show grace and forgive others, just as God shows grace and forgives you. After all of this, this head coach was able to win several games on the field at Liberty as well as take his team to several bowl games while getting his life back on track. After this great turnaround, on November 29, 2022, Coach Hugh Freeze became the 31st head coach at my alma mater, Auburn University. Although there were a lot of fans who wanted the university to hire someone else, most of the fan base was won over after Coach Freeze's introductory press conference. Despite the past, Auburn's football program showed grace by giving Coach Freeze another chance to coach in the Southeastern Conference.

Has there been a time when you did not feel like showing grace toward someone who has let you down or done you wrong?

To receive forgiveness from God, you must work on forgiving other people and showing grace toward people who you know don't deserve it. Forgiveness is a choice that you make to destroy a roadblock that stands in the way of you loving people as Christ loves you. Just as Jesus died to tear down the roadblocks caused by sin between you and God, you are required to do the same to those who have done you wrong. "But if ye forgive not men their trespasses, neither will your Father forgive your trespasses" (Matt. 6:15 KJV).

QUESTIONS

- If you answered yes to any of the Reflection Questions in the previous devotional, how can you change your thinking?
- What is your plan for walking in forgiveness, love, and grace?
- If you answered no to all the questions, how do you deal with people who display these traits?

FREEDOM FROM GUILT

Guilt can have two effects: it can either show you the problem so that you can repent and receive forgiveness, or it can rub your mistake in your face and make you feel hopeless. The enemy is known for putting guilt on people and is known as the accuser of the brethren (Rev. 12:10). How can you tell the difference between condemnation (bad for you) and conviction (good for you)? First, I'd like you to ask yourself, "Why are you feeling guilty?" Is it because you made a bad decision or have done something wrong? How can you tell if the source of your guilty feelings is God or the enemy?

God uses guilt to convict you of your sins so that you might change and make things better by receiving forgiveness, whereas the enemy uses guilt to burden you down and make you feel hopeless about what you may have done. When God convicts you, it's so that you can recognize the problem, and work on fixing it.

Whatever you are struggling with internally, you must acknowledge the issue and get the help that you need. The best way to be free from trauma that you experienced in the past or may be currently going through is to speak with a reliable source like a counselor, therapist, or a professional life coach. As a certified life coach, I have coached numerous young people and even middle-aged people who have been through trauma. I was often able to relate to the things that they were going through, since I have been through the same things. I shared my past experiences with them that caused a lot of trauma in some of my relationships with friends, family members, church members, colleagues, and business partners. I had my counselees go through a session of questions to help them recognize the problem that they had. I went over the questions and the only thing I could think of was how they shared similarities to my experiences when I went through trauma. Before that session ended, I shared our similarities of trauma and how I felt so much guilt until I was able to recognize what the problem was.

I knew I needed a mentor to counsel and guide me in the things I was doing in marketplace ministry and business. I was able to connect with and meet Pastor Sundiata Hudson at Christian Alliance of Pastors Retool, which is for leaders who are lead pastors or serve in ministry. This was held in the metro Atlanta, Georgia, area, where the visionary is Bishop Dale C. Bronner of Word of Faith Family Worship Cathedral. After developing a relationship and friendship with Pastor Hudson and other leaders within marketplace ministry, I was able to grow as a leader, businessperson, and individual.

After sharing that with my clients, they saw the need to become free from past guilt and they knew they needed someone who would walk along with them in life. That is when they were able to trust me by allowing me to be their personal success life coach.

You may feel too ashamed to discuss the guilt that you cannot seem to shake or let go of, no matter what you do or have done. Is the guilt trying to bring you to repentance and back to God, or is it trying to tell you that you cannot overcome it and bounce back in life? If you constantly feel guilty every time, recognize the problem and get the help that you may need to discuss those things that you are holding on to. God doesn't want you to stay stuck in life, nor does He tell you what a loser you are. His desire is that you may be reconciled with Him and receive forgiveness for every sin you have committed. "If we confess our sins, he is faithful and just to forgive us our sins, and to cleanse us from all unrighteousness" (1 John 1:9 KJV).

While the enemy likes to show you the mess, God wants to show you the solution. No sin is greater than another, but if your sins are forgiven and the enemy is constantly trying to make you feel guilty due to your past, you must renounce the spirit of guilt and command it to leave. No matter what the enemy tries to put in your way through other people trying to hinder you from growing daily in your personal life and spiritual journey with God, you must learn how to stay rooted and grounded in the things you are trying to accomplish in life. If you do that, you will see how the enemy will flee from you.

QUESTIONS

- What are some things that are making you feel guilty?
- Have you recognized the problem?
- What have you done to get the help you need?
- How is your spiritual journey with God?

Part 6

WE READY

GET READY

I served as lead pastor at True Life Church Tuskegee and an Associate Minister for G.O.D. Church based out of Atlanta, Georgia, with my brother Pastor Ed Long Jr. In August 2022, he kicked off a sermon series entitled "We Ready," and the God Gang leadership team broke the topic down. Each week was an eye-opener, not only to me and the leadership team of G.O.D. Church, but to everybody who tuned in. We were empowering everyone by asking this question: "Are you ready for the opposition that is heading your way and for the opportunities?"

You may have heard the phrase "Get Ready, Get Ready, Get Ready" from Bishop T.D. Jakes back in the day. I heard him use that phrase so many times, but when I was younger, I never understood what he meant by "Get Ready." He was saying that you should get ready for Yeshua, Jesus the Christ, to return, because you don't know the day or hour that He is coming back for you, but you must get ready. Jesus said in Matthew 24:44 (AMP): "Therefore, you [who follow Me] must also be ready; because the Son of Man is coming at an hour when you do not expect Him." You must also get ready for what God wants to do supernaturally in your life. What are you doing to get ready for what God wants to do in your life? If you have breath in your body and are alive, God wants you to do great things on this earth. To receive all these things from God, you must get ready every day, because you don't know when or how God is going to bless you.

QUESTIONS

- Are you ready for what God wants to do in your life?
- Who are you following? God or people?
- If Jesus were to return for you today, would you be ready?

PREPARATION

What have you been doing to prepare for Jesus' return? To prepare, you must have a personal relationship with God outside of the traditional Sunday morning worship and weekly Bible study. There are 365 days in a year; what are you doing to prepare to meet Jesus when He returns? You must learn how to act daily to prepare yourself spiritually by getting or staying connected to God. Are you also preparing yourself for what God wants to do through you to be a blessing to others? If you really want the fullness of prosperity in your life, you must learn how to bless others who are less fortunate.

True Life Church Tuskegee and G.O.D. Church are a spiritual body of believers who are living in Macon County, Alabama, and different counties in the Atlanta, Georgia, area, and around the world. As leaders in this spiritual body, we have been preparing everyone who is connected to True Life Church Tuskegee for what God is about to do next for the ministry by teaching them practical biblical principles about how God wants them to live by loving God, people, and life. G.O.D. is a Globalactic, Outreach, and Discipleship ministry. Globalactic is everywhere, because God created the world, which is our jurisdiction and domain. Outreach is where we meet people's needs, wherever they are in life. Discipleship is what God has given us as an assignment.

QUESTIONS

- If you are a spiritual leader, what are you doing to make disciples within the kingdom of God?
- Are you meeting the people's needs in your local community?
- Are you preparing people to reach their full potential of living out their life purpose?

Part 7

DEALING WITH DISCOURAGEMENT

WHY BE A HATER?

"Haters don't hate you. The reality is, they fear that they will never be able to get to where you are right now."[1]
—Leah Remillet

Haters are not going away, since they hate for no reason. These individuals have been around long before you were born. The snake in the Garden of Eden was a hater. The first recorded murderer was Cain, who killed his brother, Abel. This happened because Cain was a hater. The Pharisees and lawmakers hated Jesus and plotted to crucify Him. We all have haters, and at times have had moments where we hated people for no reason.

Hatred is a painful state. If you are honest with yourself, you know that any time you criticize someone else, it does not make you feel better about yourself. You know your position in life is out of place if you are numbered with the underachievers. Make this your last day of being a hater. What does hating get you? Give others the right to live out their life purpose so you do not hinder your growth in life.

Hatred often grows out of fear. Fear can be caused by many things, such as someone discouraging you from living out your dreams and life purpose that God has birthed inside you. The

---

1   https://quoters.info/node/623280. Accessed March 13, 2023.

Bible says, "Why are you in despair, O my soul? And why have you become restless and disturbed within me? Hope in God and wait expectantly for Him, for I shall again praise Him for the help of His presence" (Ps. 42:5 AMP). The key word in this verse is *restless*. Your purpose is not tied to other people's opinions about what God has already spoken over your life and destiny! Discouragement destroys hope, so naturally the enemy always tries to discourage you. Without hope you give up, which is exactly what the enemy wants you to do.

I'm reminded of two-time former athlete Deion Sanders, who played and won two Super Bowl titles in the National Football League (NFL) and made one World Series in the Major League Baseball (MLB). He is also an NFL Hall of Famer, and after his playing career he had a lot of ways of staying connected to the game of football. He was on sports broadcast media as an NFL analyst, then he got into coaching football while continuing to work as an NFL analyst. As he grew and climbed his way up the coaching ranks in high school, he became the twenty-first head coach of Jackson State University in the middle of a pandemic on September 21, 2020. Having been a football letterman of Florida State University under the late great head coach Bobby Bowden, Coach Sanders had no ties to Jackson State and the Southwestern Athletic Conference (SWAC). Due to COVID-19, the football season for the SWAC was pushed to the spring of 2021, where he led his team to a 4-3 record. After that short season, Coach Sanders led Jackson State to two SWAC title wins in the 2021 and 2022 seasons and two celebration bowl appearances.

During his tenure at Jackson State, Coach Sanders changed the culture for the entire Historically Black Colleges (HBCU) and Jackson State by making sure that they received coverage through ESPN for their games, and even made sure that Jackson State University players had their last name on the back of their jerseys as well as updated apparel and new practice facilities. But despite all that he did for Jackson State and the SWAC, he did not let anything or anyone who hated the success that he was having discourage him. He could have, but his hope, trust, and faith were not built on other people's opinions of him. His hope, trust, and faith were built in God.

As the 2022 regular season came to an end after the college football conference championship weekend, there was a lot of speculation that Coach Sanders was leaving Jackson State to become a power five head coach. Shortly after his team finished playing their conference championship game against Southern University, he was named the head coach of the Colorado Buffaloes football program. A lot of people were negative and upset with Coach Sanders leaving to take a power five job, and they called him all sorts of names through social media and on podcasts. But Coach Sanders never entertained their negativity. Even with all the noise from the outsiders, he stayed focused on his purpose by being positive and progressive. Even during his tenure at Jackson State, he always said that he would entertain a power five school if it was a right fit for him and his family, and God opened a door for him to become Colorado head coach.

The Bible repeatedly tells you not to be discouraged or dismayed. God knows that you will not be victorious if you get discouraged, so He always encourages you as you start out on a new assignment or task by saying to you, "Do not get discouraged." God wants you to be encouraged, not discouraged.

As kingdom citizens operating within the kingdom of God, you are to always be humble and never brag about anything, but there are others who might be jealous of your achievements. Hate and bitterness are sins, and can be brought on you by getting a new job or promotion, buying a new house, buying a new car, relationships, and even something like giving to charity. Have you worked hard, day in and day out, to get what you desired for so long, just to find out when you received that thing that it brought on haters? You must know that when God blesses you with something, it can bring on a lot of people who become jealous and hateful.

Before you receive the blessing, you must practice moving in silence. As God is shifting you to another level, you don't have to brag or post about it. We live in a world where everyone wants validation and approval from other people through social media, but if God is elevating you to another dimension in life, you don't have to post what God is currently doing in your life.

There are four types of haters:

1. There are the ones who criticize you and find fault with everything you do out of jealousy.

2. The ones who try to make you look bad in front of others.

3. The ones who purposely bring you down so you won't succeed instead of helping you.

4. And there are the haters who hate behind your back and destroy your good name with slander. Most of the time, haters are the people closest to you.

Before I became an author, empowerment speaker, entrepreneur, and philanthropist, there were a few people who were just happy with me being content, working an eight-to-five job, and pastoring. But as soon as I started operating within my gifts and talents that God had given me by being more than just a pastor and employee, these individuals began to get jealous and hate on the things that God birthed within me. I could have become discouraged, but instead I was motivated to be just as influential or more than these individuals who were jealous and hating. You might have experienced the same thing. You must stay encouraged and use your influence to inspire and motivate others to be all they can be every single day.

REFLECTIONS: ARE YOU A HATER?

Use this checklist to find out.
- ☐ I enjoy seeing others fail.
- ☐ I need to put you down to feel good about myself.
- ☐ I am the center of attention.
- ☐ I am bitter about something.
- ☐ I lose sight of contentment.

□ I stop counting my blessings and start counting the blessings of others.

□ I rarely get excited about other people's accomplishments.

□ I rarely give compliments to others.

Being a hater has no rewards. All its attributes are negative. When you're a hater, you cannot move from where you are. Decide to be glad for those who are making progress in life. If you learn how to celebrate other people's success, then people will celebrate your success. As God is elevating you in life, you must disconnect yourself from other haters and make the choice to be among winners. Successful people are always helping build each other up, while unsuccessful people are always watching your every move with jealousy. Today, make the decision to always inspire, uplift, educate, empower, and equip the ones you are connected to. Whatever profession you may serve in, learn how to get excited for your staff or players' accomplishments.

"Since we live by the Spirit, let us keep in step with the Spirit. Let us not become conceited, provoking and envying each other" (Gal. 5:25–26 NIV).

QUESTIONS

- If you answered positively or agreed with any of the statements in the Reflections, start thinking about how you can change your negative patterns.
- Are you happy for others when they get a promotion? Why, or why not?
- Are you happy when others fail? Why, or why not?
- Find ways to be happy for others when they win and succeed in life, knowing that as God did it for them, He can certainly do it for you.

ABOUT THE AUTHOR

Jay Vinson is a native of Montgomery, Alabama, and is the son of Shirley and Jimmy Vinson Sr. Jay is a licensed minister and began preaching at the age of fifteen, under the leadership of Bishop Tyrone Allen, the late Dr. Erie Allen, and his grandmother, the late Pastor Emma Dumas. A man of integrity, incredible faith, and a firm believer in the power of prayer, he knows the Word of God and preaches and teaches it with boldness and truth.

Jay is the founder of Jay Vinson Ministries Inc., based in Atlanta, Georgia. He has been featured on Praise 102.5 Atlanta's Inspiration Radio Station, Atlanta Live and Preach the Word Network, promoting his book *Stepping into Greatness from Pain to Purpose and Promise.*

Jay holds several degrees including a BA in Mass Communication from Auburn University, a Masters in Instructional Technology from the University of West Georgia, and Life Coaching from Lamad University. Distinguished honors from both universities include the Students Dean's List, Phi

Sigma Pi, National Honor Society at Auburn University, and Phi Kappa Phi, National Honor Society at University of West Georgia. Jay was also recognized as the Man of the Year for Making Headline News in 2021. Jay has been featured in several major news publications like *Yahoo Sports, Yahoo News, Vents Magazine, Digital Journal,* and the *Chicago Journal.*

In 2020 during COVID-19, Jay became a certified spiritual, youth, health and wellness life coach, author, empowerment speaker, philanthropist, and CEO of JJV Enterprises-JJV Vinson Corp. He currently lives and works in the metro Atlanta area where he is an educator, athletic coach, and athletic academic coordinator. He also has worked for the Atlanta Braves, the Gwinnett Braves, the Atlanta Falcons, University of West Georgia Football, NBCUniversal, the SEC Network, and Auburn University Athletics. Jay loves spending time with his family and friends, working out, hiking, comedy, live music, traveling, and playing and watching sports. The most important time he spends is coaching and mentoring our youth. Finally, in August of 2022, Jay launched a youth coaching academy for students and student athletes called Stepping into Greatness Youth Coaching Academy.

IF YOU ENJOYED THIS BOOK, WILL YOU HELP ME SPREAD THE WORD?

There are several ways you can help me get the word out about the message of this book...

- Post a 5-Star review on Amazon.
- Write about the book on your Facebook, Twitter, Instagram, LinkedIn – any social media you regularly use!
- If you blog, consider referencing the book, or publishing an excerpt from the book with a link back to my website. You have my permission to do this as long as you provide proper credit and backlinks.
- Recommend the book to friends – word-of-mouth is still the most effective form of advertising.
- Purchase additional copies to give away as gifts.

The best way to connect with me is by:
Facebook, Twitter, and TikTok @JayVinson30
Instagram @iamjayvinson
Email jayvinsonministriesinc@gmail.com
Phone (678) 310-6381

ENJOY THESE OTHER BOOKS BY JAY VINSON

Stepping into Greatness
From Pain to Purpose & Promise

It happens to all of us … we let the weight of the world, our hectic schedule, the demands on our jobs, our life, overwhelm us. Along the way, we get stuck in a routine. It might even be a com-

fortable routine. But deep down, inside your soul, you know you were meant for more—you were made for more!

Let this book be your pathway forward!

Through the short, easy-to-read entries, *Stepping into Greatness* will take you on a 50-day journey to exhilaration!

You can order these books from your favorite bookstores, including:

BARNES & NOBLE
amazon.com

ARE YOU READY TO STEP OUT OF YOUR MESS AND INTO YOUR DESTINY?

Then tune in to Jay Vinson's podcast for a journey to exhilaration! Find it on Apple Podcasts or Spotify.

APPLE PODCASTS

https://podcasts.apple.com/us/podcast/
stepping-into-greatness/id1546456782

SPOTIFY

https://open.spotify.com/show/5qhK0i0rCN3XAczv8oeyBX

A victorious life awaits you!

NEED A DYNAMIC SPEAKER FOR YOUR NEXT EVENT?

HOW ABOUT COACHING YOUR GROUP TO THE NEXT LEVEL OF SUCCESS?

The best way to connect with me is by:
Facebook Jay Vinson Ministries
Twitter and TikTok @JayVinson30
Instagram @iamjayvinson
Linkedin https://www.linkedin.com/in/jay-vinson-052a3253
Email jayvinsonministriesinc@gmail.com
Phone (678) 310-6381